DON MICHAEL DICIE

THE COVENTRY CAROL
(LAMENT FOR THE HOLY INNOCENTS)

OXFORD

UNIVERSITY PRESS

The Coventry Carol

Lament for the Holy Innocents

I Fl. 8' Naz. 2⅔
II Fl. 8', 4'
Pedal Soft 16', 8' coupled to II

arr. DON MICHAEL DICIE

4

Processed in the United Kingdom by
Enigma Music Production Services, Amersham, Bucks.

ISBN 978-0-19-536568-9

9 780195 365689